Advance Praise for
I Wish My Mom Was Here

"Kids often resent the loving, sometimes nagging, ways of their parents before they come around to seeing how much they actually want to be tended to. This sweet story shows the way to gratitude from a child's perspective in a way that both kids and folks can enjoy. *I Wish My Mom Was Here* is a perfect book to pull out when youngsters are yearning to be free of the yolk of parents."

—Jessica Lee Peterson, Author of *Thistles & Thorns*

"*I Wish My Mom Was Here* shows us the importance of imagination and how our families help shape our character as a person. Wonderful story with a lot of insight."

—Charlene Valdez, COTA/L Brockton Public Schools

"*I Wish My Mom Was Here* is a lovely story about wanting to escape the unpleasant shades of growing up. And learning that by doing so, we also may lose life's iridescent hues."

—Cassidy Mercer, Author of *Mad Season*

I Wish My Mom Was Here

Melissa Vigil

I Wish My Mom Was Here by Melissa Vigil, copyright © 2022 by Melissa Vigil. Author photo courtesy of the Vigil family, copyright © 2022 by the Vigil family. All illustrations, cover art design, interior layout design, and chapter head artwork © 2022 by Written Dreams Publishing.

This book is a work of fiction. All names, characters, places and events are products of the author's imagination or are used fictitiously, and any resemblance to actual persons, living or dead, or to actual places or businesses, is entirely coincidental.

All rights reserved. In accordance with the U.S. Copyright Act of 1976, no part of this publication may be reproduced, distributed, or transmitted in any form or by any means, or stored in a database or retrieval system, without prior written permission of the publisher, Written Dreams Publishing, Green Bay, Wisconsin 54311. Please be aware that if you've received this book with a "stripped" off cover, please know that the publisher and the author may not have received payment for this book, and that it has been reported as stolen property. Please visit www.writtendreams.com to send a message to the author or see more of the unique books published by Written Dreams Publishing.

Publisher/Executive Editor: Brittiany Koren
Illustrator: Arpita Saha/Amit Dey
Cover Art Designer: Ed Vincent/ENC Graphics
Print Interior Layout Designer: Amit Dey
Ebook Interior Layout Designer: Amit Dey

Category: Contemporary Fantasy Children's Fiction
Description: On his way to school, a young boy tries to make it on his own without his mom's help.
Hardcover ISBN: 978-1-951375-53-9
Paperback ISBN: 978-1-951375-54-6
Ebook ISBN: 978-1-951375-55-3
LOC Catalogue Data: Applied for.

First Edition published by Written Dreams Publishing in September 2022.
Ebook Edition published by Written Dreams Publishing in September 2022.

Green Bay, WI

Published in Green Bay, Wisconsin. Printed in the United States of America.

This book is dedicated to my mom who has always been my biggest cheerleader and taught me the art of being a mom.

And, to my husband, Alex, who made me a mom.
We lost you too soon, but your light shines bright in your three children.

I woke up in my bed to the sound of my mom's screechy voice yelling, "Get up, Fletcher. It's 7:30. You're going to be late for school."

Who cares? is what I thought.

Mom had laid clothes out on a chair for me the night before. Instead, I found my old, red t-shirt and muddy, worn sneakers and put those on. I looked in the mirror and saw my two big brown eyes staring back at me behind my slightly smudged eyeglasses. I managed to wet my dark brown hair enough so I could comb down all the parts that were sticking up.

Mom screamed up the stairs again. "Hurry up, Fletcher, and come down here so you can eat your breakfast."

I quickly brushed my teeth and went in my room to feed my hamster, Marvin. Marvin is a gray dwarf hamster. He is gray with a white belly, a fuzzy tail and big ears. He was wide awake and spinning on his wheel.

I got Marvin a year ago when I was eight. At the time, Dad said I wasn't old enough to have a pet. He said I'd forget to feed it and it would die.

After weeks of thinking and going to the library to get books about various pets, I decided on a hamster. I did hours of research about their care. I wrote a full report and gave it to my parents.

With help from my mom, we convinced my dad to let me get a hamster.

We headed to the pet store in the city. Mom gave me money to put in the parking meter before we headed inside the emporium of animals. Marvin was right up front and looking at me with pleading eyes. I knew he was the one.

It's been a year now and I've taken really good care of him—not one problem. As I stood there watching Marvin, I was interrupted once again by Mom's scream insisting I was late. She sounded really mad this time.

I rode the banister down the stairs in my house, even though Mom always tells me not to because I might break my neck.

I know she's probably right, but it's sooooo fun, so it's worth the risk in my book.

As I stepped into the kitchen, Mom immediately began to sigh and rub her forehead. She asked, "Why do you always have to be so pokey?"

In my head, I could think of a million excuses for being "pokey," but since I wasn't in the mood for arguing, I just muttered, "Sorry."

She always says she should've named me DillyDally. I wonder what makes moms so crabby. Maybe there's a crabby mom flu that goes around.

I wish I knew what medicine to give my mom. Whenever I'm sick, she takes the best care of me. She knows what medicine to give me, wraps me in warm blankets, puts a cool cloth on my head, and makes me her special soup until I feel better.

Mom placed a bowl of oatmeal heaped with blueberries on the table in front of the chair where I sit every morning.

When I visit Grandma's house, I get the newest sugary cereal on the market. Mom shakes her head whenever I ask her to add that to her shopping list and tells me growing kids need a healthy breakfast every day.

She added, "Eat quick," and tossed me a spoon.

As soon as I was done eating, I grabbed my backpack and coat, and got ready to leave.

Mom came into the kitchen with a wool hat in her hand as I was about to head out the door. "Fletcher, please take this hat with you. The weather is getting colder."

I would have told her I was too big for hats and then slammed the door, but I still wasn't in the mood for arguing. Instead, I muttered, "Fine" and ran out the door.

Normally, I take my bike to school, but the other day the chain broke and Mom was planning on fixing it for me today.

As I walked down the driveway, I heard the door open behind me.

Two seconds later, Mom yelled, "If you ever wear that raggedy red shirt and those awful sneakers to school again, you're grounded."

She also reminded me to come home right after school because I had promised the neighbor I would rake up their leaves today. I had put up flyers a few months ago advertising my ability to pull weeds, rake, and do other yard chores. I've made quite a bit of money and I'm saving it in my new piggy bank.

As my feet pounded against the pavement, the gears in my brain began to churn. Instead of following this sidewalk to school, as I did every day, I thought of running away.

The sidewalk led me to the jungle where I was a big-game hunter and carried a bow and arrow with me at all times. I was free, and there was no one there to yell at me.

I made friends with the monkeys and took showers from water sprayed by the elephants. The sounds in the jungle were like music to my ears. The colors of the plants and flowers were like none that I had ever seen. It was a great life until I got hungry.

I couldn't make those bananas fall down from that tall, towering tree. I tried shaking the tree, but it wouldn't budge.

I wish my mom was here to help me.

Next, I tried climbing the tree but only managed to get a few feet before sliding back down. I attempted it a few more times because Mom always says "never give up." I still didn't have any luck.

I looked for other food closer to the ground, but nothing looked familiar. Mom always told me not to eat things that I don't know what they are.

Finally, I gave up and sat next to a lion drinking from a pond. I was really hungry.

I wish my mom was here to make me something to eat.

The jungle was no place for me, so I left and journeyed to the Arctic.

In the snowy mountains, I was a powerful dogsled racer. The dogs and I pushed the sled around all day practicing for the big race. The dogs were Siberian Huskies with fluffy, gray and white fur. They were so smart and quickly learned my commands of "Haw" and "Gee" for turning left and right. Sometimes, we would rest, eat, and play in the snow together. Life was great until I got cold. My ears, hands, and feet started to get numb. I tried rubbing my hands together and jumping up and down to get warm, but nothing helped.

I wish my mom was here to give me a warm hat, scarf, and mittens.

The Arctic was too cold for me, so I travelled to the oceanside to try my luck at deep-sea fishing. Perhaps I could hook a kingfish or shark.

I sat on the end of the dock and dropped my fishing line. I didn't get many bites, but that's okay. I probably wouldn't have been able to reel up anything too heavy anyway.

When the sun got too hot, I jumped in the water to swim and dive with the dolphins.

I darted in and out of the coral reefs as I played tag with the swordfish.

Everything was going great until…one day on the dock an older man came up to me and said, "You're too young to be a deep-sea fisherman. You'll have to get off this dock."

No fair.

I wish my mom was here to tell him I was old enough. She always sticks up for me.

I yelled good-bye to the dolphins and headed for the Rocky Mountains.

The weather was perfect—bright sunshine with a tiny breeze to ease the heat. There was a peaceful silence as I climbed the steep mountainside.

In the distance, I saw red-tailed hawks and heard coyotes howl as they sang out to me, cheering me on to the top. Everything was calm. Certainly, there was no one here to yell at me. I considered living here for the rest of my life.

Would Mom miss me?

As I reached up and moved closer to the top, my left foot slipped and I slid down the mountainside. I heard pebbles tumbling along the side of me as they broke off from the larger rock formations and created distant echoes as they plummeted to the bottom.

My heart raced as I lost control, falling faster.

Suddenly, I reached out my hand and grabbed a rock stuck out from the mountain. I gripped it hard and held on tight.

I instantly came to a stop. I had never been so scared before in my whole life.

I wish my mom was here to comfort me. She would have told me that the mountain was too dangerous to climb.

I decided to try something I knew I was good at. Bike racing.

I headed to France to race in the biggest bike race in the world, the Tour de France. I always beat my neighbor Toby to the park, so I figured I had a pretty good shot at winning. I grabbed my shiny, green bike plastered with superhero stickers and headed to the starting line with over a hundred other racers. Millions of spectators lined the streets anticipating the beginning of the race. My confidence soared as I envisioned the finish line with a medal around my neck.

The gun fired signaling the start of the race. The crowd went wild with cheering and everyone was taking pictures. I dug into my bike pedals with all my might and started propelling forward at a rapid speed.

Ten feet into the race, the chain on my bike broke and the rest of the bicyclists blew past me.

I wish my mom was here to fix my chain.

Since I didn't have any luck with bike racing, I decided to head to New York City.

My mom has taught me how to save money, so I think working at a big fancy bank would be right up my alley.

I drove a bright red sports car through the heart of downtown. Skyscrapers soared over me, cars were honking nonstop. People were everywhere. I could smell hot dogs on the street corners. Everything seemed so exciting and filled me with energy.

After an hour of looking, I finally found an empty parking space. I got out and realized I didn't have any money with me to put in the parking meter.

I wish my mom was here to give me some coins.

I quickly ran into the bank and asked to speak to the manager. When she appeared, I explained that I was looking for a job.

She looked me up and down and shook her head. "Sorry," the lady said, "we require our employees to wear suits and ties. A raggedy red t-shirt and worn sneakers will never do."

I wish my mom was here. She would have laid out a nice outfit for me.

I walked back out to my car, but unfortunately, it had been towed away.

I decided the only place left for me to go was outer space.

We had been studying the planets in school and I was sure this was the place for me. I headed to NASA and boarded the next available spaceship.

Inside, I found my space suit, a lot of control panels, and a cabinet full of special astronaut food. I had everything I needed. I radioed down to the station and told them I was ready!

I heard the countdown of "3-2-1" and was then blasted upwards at alarming speed. I watched the ground quickly disappear as I shot through the clouds.

I travelled into the dark world surrounded by planets, stars, and other large rocks suspended in the air. Comets zoomed by the window. I was in utter amazement by the beauty. I had no doubt that this was the most perfect place for me.

And then, I started to feel sick.

My stomach began to feel queasy and I felt dizzy.

I wish my mom was here. She would know what medicine to give me, take care of me, and make me feel better.

The sick feeling only continued to get worse, and I knew I really needed my mom.

"Fletcher? Why are you walking so slow? Don't you know you're going to be late for school? Here, hop in," Mom called out. She had driven up next to me in her car.

I don't think I'd ever been so happy to see her in all my life. I jumped in with a smile and we headed to school.

I had a minute to spare when we arrived. I'm lucky I have a mom or I would have been late for school. She is always looking out for me, making sure I'm fed, dressed appropriately, and not doing something dangerous. Most of all, she believes in me.

I leaned over and kissed my mom good-bye. Then, I told her how much I loved her.

"I love you, too," Mom said, and hugged me back.

As I walked into school, I was glad my mom was here to help me. I was so lucky to have her as my mom.

Acknowledgements

Thank you to my wonderful children, Iris, Bency, and Cesar, for their support and understanding when Mom had to work on her book, and for giving feedback.

Thank you to the team at Written Dreams Publishing for believing in *I Wish My Mom Was Here*, and to the talented Arpita Saha for her wonderful illustrations.

And a very special thank you to all of my readers. I hope you enjoyed Fletcher's story.

About the Author

Melissa Vigil is a mom to three children. When she is not busy running her kids to various activities, you can find her creating art of all kinds, hiking through the woods, entangled in a heated game of croquet or Risk, or lost in a good book in Freedom, Wisconsin.

Melissa has always held a deep appreciation for children's books and realizes the importance they play in a young person's life. She created many books at home when her children were very young for their personal use to help them learn and understand new concepts. Melissa lost her husband to pancreatic cancer in 2018. She and her young children have found throwing themselves into the things they love the most helps them deal with that great loss. Sometimes, it is just as simple as snuggling up together and reading a good children's book. *I Wish My Mom Was Here* is her first children's fiction novel.

CPSIA information can be obtained
at www.ICGtesting.com
Printed in the USA
BVHW012102211022
649988BV00006B/334